THE VISION OF ARIDÆUS

BY G. R. S. MEAD

1907

THE VISION OF ARIDÆUS

PREAMBLE.

The Story of Aridæus is the most detailed and graphic Vision of Hades preserved to us from classical antiquity, and exceeds in interest even Plato's Story of Er and Cicero's Dream of Scipio, not to speak of the less known Visions of Krates and of Zosimus.

It brings to a striking conclusion the instructive treatise of Plutarch, the Greek title of which may be rendered, *On the Delay of the Deity in Punishing the Wicked* or *On the Delay of Divine Justice*.

Plutarch of Chæroneia, in Bœotia, flourished in the last quarter of the second century (? 50-120 A.D.). He was one of the most enlightened of the ancients, exceedingly well versed in the details of the religious philosophies and the sciences of his day, and possessed of good critical abilities; he was also a man of wide religious experience, holding high office at Delphi in the service of Apollo and also in connection with the Dionysiac Rites, and had a profound knowledge of the inner grades of the Osiric Mysteries. He was educated in Athens and Alexandria and lectured at Rome.

Plutarch is one of our most valuable sources of information on the Hellenic and Hellenistic theology, theosophy and mystagogy of the first century, and is therefore indispensable in any comparative study of the Gnosis.

Our philosopher has been variously styled a Platonist, Neo-platonist, Eclectic, Ethicist and Syncretist; but it is very difficult to label Plutarch precisely, for as Dr. John Oakesmith, in his instructive essay, *The Religion of Plutarch: A Pagan Creed of Apostolic Times* (London; 1902), says, he "suggested a frame of mind rather than inculcated a body of dogma." He was in some ways a very good specimen of what we ought to mean to day by the term theosophist.

Though there is not a single word in the whole of his voluminous writings to show that he was acquainted with Christianity, it has nevertheless been argued that he must have derived his ethics and monotheistic ideas from Christianity; and, curiously enough, Dr. Charles Super, in his *Between Heathenism and Christianity* (Chicago; 1889), selects the very treatise of Plutarch's which contains our Vision (together with Seneca's *Concerning Providence*), to demonstrate the intimate points of contact between the religio-philosophy of the time and the New Religion.

We have, however, shown at length in the Prolegomena of *Thrice Greatest Hermes* that the doctrines of Hellenistic theology, theosophy and gnosis were widespread in the first century, and had in many ways a common language with the books of the New Testament writers; there is, however, no question of direct plagiarism on either side.

The Vision of Aridæus is of interest in many ways, and doubtless that interest would be increased for us if we could be persuaded with Count Joseph de Maistre, that "it is permissible to believe that Dante took the general idea of his Inferno" from the description of the punishments in our Vision, as de Maistre writes in his translation of the treatise

(Paris; 1856). I must, however, leave the suggestion to Dante scholars, with the remark that it is now proved, especially by the work of Dr. J. E. Sandys, that the Renaissance of classical studies began, long before the capture of Constantinople, in the days of Petrarch and Boccaccio.

Concerning the source and composition of the Vision, and how Plutarch intended us to take it, as many opinions may be held as in the case of the better-known Vision of r in Plato. I would, however, myself suggest that the key to the situation is to be found in the following passage of our philosopher-mystagogue:

"When a man dies he goes through the same experiences as those who have their consciousness increased in the Mysteries. Thus in the terms teleut©n ('to die') and tele<sqai ('to be initiated') we have an exact correspondence, word to word and fact to fact.

"First of all there are wanderings and wearying journeyings and paths on which we look with suspicion, and that seem to have no end; then, before the end, every kind of terror, shuddering, trembling, sweating, stupor.

"But at last a marvellous light shines out to meet us, pure spots and far fields welcome us, with song and dance and the solemnities of sacred sounds and holy sights.

"In which state he who has already perfected himself in all things and received initiation, reaches his full freedom, and passing everywhere at will, receives the crown, and accomplishes his mystery, in communion with the holy and pure; gazing down upon the unpurified multitude of the uninitiated who are still in life, wallowing in the deep mire and mist, and herded together below him, abiding in misery from fear of death and want of faith in the blessedness of the soul-life.

"For you should know that the intercourse and conjunction of the soul with body is contrary to nature." (Plut., *Fragm.* v. 9, ed. Didot).

The further consideration of this suggestion, however, will more conveniently come later, when the reader has become acquainted with the Vision.

The treatise is in the form of a Platonic dialogue. The persons of the dialogue are: Plutarch himself, who is the chief speaker; Patrocleas, his son-in-law; Timon, his brother; and Olympichus, an intimate friend. The scene is the Portico of the Temple of Apollo at Delphi. The tract is addressed to a certain Quintus, who must have been a Roman, but of whom nothing further is known.

In the course of his argument, Plutarch remarks that no punishment is more distressing and makes us more ashamed than to see our children suffering through our misdeeds. And if the soul of an impious law-breaker could after death see his children or friends or family in great adversity because of him and paying the penalty of his misdeeds, no one would ever be able to persuade him, even for the wealth of Zeus, to be unjust or licentious again on his return to earth.

"I could tell you a true story (*logos*) which I lately heard," he continues, "but I'm afraid you would think it a tale (*mythos*); I therefore confine myself to probability only."

As, however, the others pressed for the story, Plutarch replied: "Permit me first to finish the argument as to probabilities, and then, if you like, I will set the tale going, if indeed it be a tale."

Plutarch here evidently intends it to be understood that for him the story is *logos* and not *mythos*; and by *logos* he means as evidently that it is based on "fact" and not "probability."

This is plain from his own words, and is further strengthened by the general use at that date of the word *logos* for a serious narrative, especially a "sacred discourse," or a story of initiation.

It is further of interest to note that Plato at the end of his story of the Vision of Er refers to it as a *mythos*. Can Plutarch have had this in mind, and does he wish to draw a distinction between *his* "logos" and the famous "myth" of Plato?

It is more than probable that the myths of Plato had been frequently discussed in the schools, and that there were very various opinions as to how they were to be taken; the term *myth* had fallen into disrepute among the learned, and Plutarch here as elsewhere uses *logos* as a better description of a narrative connected with the doctrines of initiation.

Plutarch tells us that the hero of his story was a certain Aridæus of Soli, a town on the sea-coast of Asia Minor; he was an intimate friend of Protogenes of Tarsus (Plut., *On Love*, ii.) who stayed with Plutarch for some time at Delphi. Aridæus related his experiences to Protogenes and other intimate friends; and so we may suppose that Plutarch first heard the story from Protogenes, and finding it somewhat in keeping with what he himself had been taught, or seen dramatically represented, in one or other of the initiatory-rites through which he had passed, he polished it up and amplified it to suit his purpose.

This Aridæus had lived a notorious life of great profligacy and villainy; he was a sort of millionaire scoundrel of the period. Report had it that on his sending to ask the Oracle of Amphilochus, at Mallus in Cilicia, whether there was any chance of his living a better life for the rest of his days, he received the reply that he would do better when he was dead.

Shortly after, Aridæus had a severe fall, and though he broke no bones, the shock did for him. Three days later, just as they were about to bury him, he recovered consciousness. After this unpleasant experience, Aridæus became an entirely reformed character, of quite exemplary virtue. Such a startling change could not pass unnoticed; but it was only to a few of his greatest friends that he told what had happened to him during the "three days." The story runs as follows: THE VISION.

When his consciousness passed out of the body, he experienced from the change the same sort of sensation that a sailor would who had been swept overboard into deep water. Then, coming up a little, he seemed to breathe in every part of him, and to see on every side at once, as though the soul--the "single eye"--had been opened.

Of objects with which he had been previously familiar, he saw none save the stars; they were, however, of stupendous size and at enormous distances from one another, and poured forth a marvellous radiance of colour and sound, so that the soul riding smoothly in the light, as a ship in calm weather, sailed easily and swiftly in every direction.

Omitting most of the things he saw, he said that the souls of the dead, in passing from below upwards, formed a flame-like bubble from which the air was excluded; then the bubble quietly broke, and they came forth with men-like forms and well-knit frames. They, however, differed in their movements; some leaped out with wonderful lightness and darted straight up; but others kept turning round together in a circle, like spindles, bobbing up and down, with a mixed and confused motion, which recovered its balance only after a long time and with great difficulty.

As to the majority of them, he did not know who they were; he recognized, however, two or three acquaintances, and tried to join them and enter into conversation. They, however, neither heard him, nor were they themselves. Demented and panic-stricken, avoiding every look and touch, they first turned round and round by themselves; then, falling in with many in the same condition, they huddled together, drifting about in every direction confusedly, with no object in view, and uttering meaningless shouts, like war-cries, intermingled with wails and screams of fear.

Other souls, however, were to be seen above at the top of the envelope [or surround] shining with joy, frequently approaching one another in friendly intercourse but avoiding the troubled souls below them. They seemed to show their dislike by drawing themselves together into themselves, and their joy and delight by expansion and extension.

In that region, he said, he saw only one soul of a relative, though he was not quite sure about it, for his kinsman had died while he (Aridæus) was still a boy. However, he came up to him and said: "Welcome, Thespesius!" And on his replying in surprise that his name was not Thespesius, but Aridæus, the other remarked:

"It *was* Aridæus, but from henceforth it will be Thespesius [that is, 'Sent by the Gods']; for indeed thou art not dead, but by the will of the Gods thou art come hither with thy reason about thee, whilst thou hast left the rest of thy soul, as it were an anchor, in the body. And this thou mayest now and hereafter prove to thyself by the fact that the souls of the dead cast no shadow and never close their eyelids."

On hearing this, Thespesius set himself the more to use his rational faculties, and taking a closer look he saw that he had a faint and shadowy outline attached to him, while they [the dead] shone all round and were transparent, though not all in the same way. For some were like the purest full-moon light, emitting one smooth, continuous and even colour; while others had patches across them or narrow strips. Others again were quite mottled--extraordinary sights--dappled with livid spots, like adders; and others had faint scratches.

Then Thespesius' kinsman (for there is nothing to prevent our calling souls by persons' names) pointed out everything telling him that Adrasteia, daughter of Necessity and Zeus, had been set in highest heaven to administer retribution for all offences; and no sinner was either great enough or small enough to escape her by force or avoid her vigilance.

"There are three kinds of punishment he continued, "each appropriate to one of the warders and executors [of Adrasteia]. For speedy Punishment (Poin') deals with those who are chastized at once, in the body and through their bodies, but in somewhat mild fashion, since many offences are passed over as requiring purification only. In the case of those, however, whose moral cure is a more serious business, they are handed over by their conscience (lit. *daimÇ n*) to Justice (Dik') after their decease. And finally, in the case of those who are rejected by Justice as altogether incurable, Fury, (Erinys) the third and most implacable of Adrasteia's ministers, pursues them as they wander and flee, some one way, some another, and pitifully and cruelly undoes them all and thrusts them down into a state of which we can neither speak nor think.

"Of these [three] kinds of correction," he said, "that which is effected by Punishment, while a man is still alive, resembles a method of chastisement in vogue with the Persians, among others, when they strip the clothes and headresses off the culprits and scourge the former, while the latter entreat them with tears to stop. In like manner, punishments by means of loss of goods and bodily suffering do not really probe the disease sharply nor reach vice itself, but for the most part touch only the reputations and sensibilities of the culprits.

"Accordingly whenever a man leaves that world for this unpunished and impure, Justice grips him by the soul just as he is, naked, unable to put anything on, and so hide and cloak his villainy, but every bit of him in full view of every one on all sides.

"And first of all he is shown to his good parents, if such they are, or to his ancestors, as an object of loathing and a disgrace to the family; whereas if his forebears are bad, he has to look on their punishments and they on his; and this continues for a long time, until he has exhausted every one of his evil tendencies in pain and toil, which in extent and intensity as much exceed all suffering in the body, as waking consciousness is more vivid than a dream. And the scars and marks of every one of their evil tendencies more or less remain on all of them.

"Observe," he continued, "the colours of the souls of every shade and sort: that greasy brown-grey is the pigment of sordidness and selfishnes; that blood-red inflamed shade is a sign of a savage and venomous nature; wherever blue-gray is, from such a nature incontinence in pleasure is not easily eradicated; innate malignity with envy, causes that livid discoloration in the same way as cuttle-fish eject their sepia.

"Now it is in earth-life that the vice of the soul (being acted upon by the passions and reacting upon the body) produces these discolorations; while the purification and correction here have for their object the removal of these blemishes, so that the soul may become entirely ray-like (*augoeid' s*) and of uniform colour.

"As long as these colours are present, there are relapses into the passions, accompanied with pulsings and throbbings; with some souls faint and soon suppressed, but with others vigorously intensified.

"Of these, some by dint of repeated correction at length recover their proper disposition and condition; others again, by the strength of their intractability and their being nailed down to the love of pleasure, are carried down to the bodies of beasts.

"The former, through weakness of reason and inertia of the contemplative principle, are carried down by the practical element to birth [as men]; while the latter, lacking an instrument for their unbridled lust, long to unite desires to enjoyment and bring these together by means of [any] body,--for out of body there is only an imperfect shadow and dream of pleasure without fulfilment."

After these explanations he was conducted by his guide at great speed across an immense space, as it seemed, nevertheless easily and directly as though supported by wings of light-rays, until, having arrived at a vast vortex extending downwards, he was abandoned by the power which supported him.

He observed also that the same thing happened to the rest of the souls there; for checking their flight, like birds, and sinking down, they fluttered round the vortex in a circle, not daring to go straight through it.

Inside it seemed to be decked, like Bacchic Caves, with trees and verdure and every kind of foliage; while out of it there breathed a soft and gentle air, laden with marvellous sweet scents, making a blend like wine for topers, so that the souls feasting on the perfume were melted with delight in mutual embraces, while the whole place was wrapt in revelry and laughter and the spirit of sport and pleasure.

Thespesius' guide told him that this was the way by which Dionysus ascended to the Gods and afterwards took up Semelʻ ; it was called the Place of Oblivion (Lʻ thʻ).

Therefore he would not suffer Thespesius to stay there, though he wished to do so, but forcibly dragged him away; explaining how that the rational element of the soul was melted and moistened by pleasure, while the irrational and that which tends to body being thus moistened and made fleshly, awakens the memory of the body, and from this memory comes a yearning and desire which drag down the soul into generation, . . . the soul-being weighed down with moisture.

Then Thespesius, after taking another journey as great as the former one, seemed to see in the distance a huge basin, with streams flowing into it: one whiter than the foam of the sea or snow; another like the purple which the rainbow sends forth; while others were tinged with other colours, each at a distance having its own splendour.

But when they came closer, the basin itself (the surroundings disappearing and the colours growing fainter) lost its varied colouring and retained only a white brilliance. And he saw three beings (*daimones*) seated together, forming a triangle one with the other, mixing the streams in definite proportions.

Thespesius' soul-guide thereupon informed him that Orpheus had advanced as far as this when he went in search of the soul of his wife, but, through not remembering correctly, had spread an erroneous report that the Oracle at Delphi was shared by Apollo and Night, whereas Apollo had nothing to do with Night.

"But that which you see," he said, "is the common oracle of Night and Sel‘ n‘ , which eventuates nowhere on the earth in one particular seat, but meanders in every direction manwards in visions and images. It is from this that dreams, after being mixed, as you see, spread abroad a mixture of the simple and true with the complex and fallacious.

"As for the Oracle of Apollo," he continued, "you have not seen it, nor will you be able to do so, for the stern-cable of your soul does not give or slacken further upwards, but drags it down through being made fast to the body."

At the same time his guide brought him closer and tried to show him the light which streamed from the Tripod, as he explained, through the Bosom of Themis and rested upon Parnassus. But though he longed to see, he could not because of the dazzling nature of the light. As he passed, however, he caught a woman's high voice in rhythmic verse prophesying among other things apparently the time of his own death.

His genius (*daimÇn*) told him that this was the voice of the Sibyl, who sings of things to come as she circles in the face of the Moon. He would therefore have liked to hear more, but was driven in the opposite direction by the Moon's impetus, as in the eddies of a whirlpool. So he heard but little, but that little contained a prophecy about Mount Vesuvius and the destruction of Dicæarcheia by fire, and a scrap about the reigning Emperor, which ran:

"Being good, by sickness will he leave his throne."

After this they turned back to see the punishments. And first of all nothing but distressing and pitiful sights met their eyes; till suddenly Thespesius, without at all expecting it, came across his own friends, kinsfolk and intimates in torment; and they in their terrible sufferings and unseemly and painful chastisements lamented and wept aloud to him.

And last of all he looked down upon his own father emerging from some sort of a pit, covered with marks and scars, stretching out his hands to him; he was no longer allowed to keep silence, but compelled by the authorities to confess that his hands were stained with the blood of some wealthy strangers he had poisoned. On earth he had completely succeeding in escaping detection, but in the after-state all was brought home to him; for part of his crimes he had already been punished, but for the rest he had still to suffer.

But so great were Thespesius' consternation and terror, that he dared not intercede or entreat for his father. When, however, he would have turned and fled, he could no longer see his gentle and familiar guide, but was thrust forward by others of terrifying appearance, and as though there were no choice but to go through with the business.

Thus he had to see that the shades of those who were known to be bad and had been punished in earth-life, did not get such a dressing, as they had already done hard labour for their irrational and passionate natures; whereas those who had passed their lives in undetected vice, under cloak and show of virtue, were forced by those who surrounded them, to turn their souls inside out in throes of pain, wriggling in unnatural contortions, just as sea-polyps turn themselves inside out after swallowing the hook.

Some of these they flayed, and peeling off their skins showed them covered with spots and festering sores, owing to the diseased condition of their rational and ruling principle. Others, he said, he saw entwined like snakes, two, three, or more together, malevolently devouring one another in revenge for what they had suffered or done to each other while living.

There were further [three] lakes alongside one another: one of boiling-hot gold; one of lead, bitterly cold; another of iron, terribly hard. And there were dæmons on duty, who, just like smiths with tongs, put in and took out the souls of those who suffered from the vice of insatiable greed and avarice.

After they had been made red-hot and transparent by firing them in the gold lake, they thrust them into the lead one and gave them a bath in it; and after they had been frozen there and made as hard as hail, they further transferred them into the lake of iron; there they became terribly black, and after being smashed up by its hardness and crushed to atoms, they changed their shapes. They were then in this state taken back to the gold lake, suffering, he said, terrible agonies in their transformations. But the most pitiable sufferings of all, Thespesius declared, were those of the souls who, when they seemed to have at last got their discharge from Justice, were arrested again. These were the souls of those whose crimes had been visited on their children or descendants.

For whenever one of the latter happened to come up, he fell upon the criminal in a rage, crying out against him and showing him the marks of his sufferings, reproaching him and pursuing after him. And though he tried to get away and hide himself, he could not; for the chastizers speedily hunted them back to Justice and constrained them all over again, in spite of their pitiful cries for mercy owing to what they already knew of the punishments in store.

And to some of them, he said, many of the souls of their descendants attached themselves, just like bees or bats, crowding thick upon each other, and gibbering in anger at the memory of what they had suffered through them. Last of all he saw the souls [of this class] who were returning to birth, being forcibly turned into all sorts of beasts, having their shapes changed by the shapers of animals, with blows of curious instruments. In some cases they hammered the whole of their parts together; in others they twisted them back, and some parts they planed off smooth, and got rid of them entirely, so that they might be fitted to other habits and modes of life.

Among them he saw the soul of Nero in a bad state generally and pierced with red-hot nails. The smiths had in hand for it the form of Pindar's viper, in which it would be conceived and come to life by gnawing itself through its mother.

Hereupon, he said, a great light suddenly shone forth, and a voice from the light was heard giving orders to change it into a milder type, and devise a creature that croaks round marshes and lakes; he had been already punished for his crimes, and now some favour was due to him from the Gods for having freed Greece, the most excellent nation of his subjects and the one dearest to the Gods.

This was as far as Thespesius got in his vision. When, however, he was going to turn back, he had a most terrible fright; for a woman of amazing form and size seized hold of him, with the words: "Come thou to me so that thou mayest the better remember the details"; and she was just going to use on him a red-hot stylus, like [encaustic] painters, when another woman stopped her.

Then, as though he were suddenly sucked through a tube by a terribly strong and violent in-breath, he lit in his body, and woke up just as they were on the point of burying him.

COMMENTS.

The consideration of this story of vision opens up so many important questions that the main difficulty is to compress within the limits of this small volume a portion of what might be written. I shall therefore attempt to touch on some of the more general points of interest only.

We first notice that the consciousness of the soul passes from what we may call the plane of "earth" to that of "water"; and it is probably from this, which seems to be a somewhat general fact of psychic experience, that the glyphs of "water," "sea," "ocean," etc., have been adopted so widely as symbolic of subtle matter.

In this state souls may be said to "sail about," because apparently there is no motion of limbs; their "astral" vehicle is conveyed by the current; they sail about on sound- or light-waves, perceiving no ordinary physical mind-forms, but "stars," certain magnitudes, or perhaps "nodes," where certain greater currents meet. Or, if we must interpret this sublime spectacle in a more physical sense, it may be said to pertain to the region beyond the lower earth-atmosphere where sight is unobscured by that atmosphere.

The "single eye" is a Platonic term.

The "flame-like bubble" vehicling the souls of the dead is a graphic phrase that reminds us admirably of all we have heard of what has been called in modern theosophy the "auric envelope."

But why is the "air" said to be excluded from it? If it is permissible to lay stress on the point, I would suggest that it is because what is called here "air," in connection with what has been previously called "earth" and "water," is that which brings with it proper self-consciousness. "Fire," "water," and "earth" play together to make the "forms." If the "bubbles" had had "air" in them, they would have been fully developed proper souls, capable of looking at themselves, considering and studying themselves from without personality. The "bubbles" thus pertain to a lower state of development, namely, the "watery spheres."

But I fear that this mode of interpretation may perhaps prove slightly perplexing, and I will therefore not pursue it. It need only be added, to complete the idea for those who choose to follow it up for themselves, that it might be said that every one at death delivers over something, and then reappears in his own true inner form. Those who "darted straight up" to the higher "air," would thus be those who were able to retain with themselves something outside personality.

"Air," in this sense would be outside personality, and we need something within ourselves to correspond, to attract us "up" to these more transcendent states of consciousness.

To keep more closely to our text; the vision here seems to describe in graphic fashion the difference between souls that are balanced and souls that are unbalanced; the former pass to a state of calm, if not of equilibrium, and the latter remain in the swirling currents of the lower emotional nature, the currents or streams in the great emotional sea, on the waves of which they drift rather than sail. Its state is determined by whether the soul's consciousness is centered in a properly built formal or completely human mind or in an embryonic or animal-human mind. In Greek terms, these states or habitats are called Elysium and Hades; or, if we please, the higher and lower Hades or Invisible.

The state of the less developed souls is well depicted by our vision, for numerous seers in our own day agree in stating that many of those who die are either in great fear owing to the soul-paralyzing doctrine of an eternal hell, or are all-distraught at the strange and unexpected nature of their surroundings, being aware of neither where they are nor what is expected of them.

Our seer tried to talk to them, but they avoided him. This is apparently more or less true at all times and in all places under such circumstances; for Aridæus being still alive, and being under special favour, or "the will of the Gods," had his consciousness out-turned, whilst theirs was in-turned. And in general it may be said that people who are selfish and live centered on themselves, will never pay attention when higher intelligencies speak to them. Fear is another characteristic of souls in this state; they always think external forces are going to injure them. This is presumably because it stops their own self-meditation, which is their only idea of happiness.

The envelope or surround that contained Elysium and Hades was thought of by the ancients as extending "as far as the moon"; for they generally thought of the after-death state from a purely objective physical standpoint. The "moon" was thus the physical moon, and the sublunary regions were the earth's atmosphere as far as the moon.

Mystically the sublunary are the states "ruled by the Moon," the Mystic Mother who weaves the silver ghosts that dance round all, up to a certain stage in evolution, when the Sun of the true mind shines forth with golden rays.

With regard to souls in the higher portions of the surround, the Elysian state *proper* or higher heaven-world, the unselfish outward-looking characteristic of mind always brings joy, radiant joy, which in its fairest modes may well be thought to go forth so as to benefit all the world. There should always be a large capacity for such joy in any soul that is really and truly thus turned outward and is growing fast. Such souls expand to show joy; this expansion connotes at the same time, adhering and clinging to the beloved object. The two expand till they embrace and interpenetrate; for love interpenetrates.

The change of name from Aridæus to Thespesius is to be noted. Change of name is found in almost all initiatory rites, and corresponds to an inner change of power. In the mystery-language of the Greeks, the epopt may be said to meet with the psychopomp; the soul meets with a more ancient kinsman belonging to the family of its higher self.

The soul of Aridæus was still attached to the body by a link, which when translated into terms of physical vision appeared as a cord. This has been very frequently seen by seers; it corresponds with the umbilical cord of the child. There is apparently a corresponding connection between any two vehicles of man's consciousness; but whereas on the physical plane it is a cord, on other planes it would be better, perhaps, to think of it as a super-physical (magnetic, psychic, mental, etc.) connection.

Aridæus is next told to notice that the souls of the dead never close their eyelids. And it has been remarked by many that "ghosts" and apparitions of the dead never do so. The natural closing of the eyes is normally conditioned in our world by alternations of light and darkness, depending on the revolution of the earth; but in the subtle state of matter, where the solid earth does not intervene to shut out the sunlight, the realm of the "astral light," there are no alternations of light and darkness.

It is said that the Gods never close their eyes, and there is also an apocryphal legend that tells us the same of Jesus. The "shadow," again, which Aridæus throws owing to his still being alive and not one of the dead, is presumably some portion of subtle physical matter which clouds his psychic envelope, in that he was still "anchored" to his body, by means of what we may call a psycho-physical magnetic current.

Mystically it may be said that while the physical external sun casts a shadow, when we are our own Sun, we do not cast a shadow.

Again mystically it may be said that it is the mind in man which casts shadow and gives position relative to the inward Sun.

The "dead," again in this connection, may also mean those who have retired right out of the physical and mental form and are struggling in either the lower or higher soul-state.

It is said that there are states of subtle matter analogous to the solid, liquid and gaseous states of the physical, synthesized by a fourth, the etheric; or again, the earthy, watery, airy, fiery states, synthesized by the fifth, or quintessence, according to the immemorial scheme of the four elements; or again of seven, perhaps by a duplication of the first category.

After death, it is said, the soul, or rather the psychic envelope, passed through corresponding stages, gradually shedding off the denser phases and becoming more and more ethereal. This subtle matter and all of its phases are luminiferous, and with this in mind it is easy to follow the idea of the light-colours playing over and through the soul-envelope, and to understand how they are of different radiance according to the phase of substance which is dominant in this subtle envelope.

The majority of humans, it is said, spend most of their after-death existence in such conditions. But it would seem that the intermediary state and the heaven-state are conditioned by modes of motion rather than by form. I can well believe that we do not die in order to live in another kind of a prison-house of a subtle body of form, but rather that we die to experience the exact opposite of what we experience on earth, to be turned as it were "inside out," to revivify ourselves, to live in a state where form is ever interchangeable and power or life is the law or rule or guiding principle.

Most people, if we can believe our text is based upon a foundation of true vision, are carried about on the psychic streams; those who have built themselves a formal mind preserve their balance, and sail about in the sea very happily; those whose mentality is only slightly developed and have no right tendencies, wobble about, so to speak, and get somewhat giddy, we may suppose.

More advanced souls who have built themselves what is called a "formless" mind, enter the spiritual state. We cannot, I believe, get there without a "formless" mind, for we must have some mind there for experience; for it is by mind that the psychic is changed to the spiritual state. It is mind in its widest sense that mystically alters for the individual the direction of the ceaseless ever-flowing psychic into the self-centralization and all-directions of the spiritual. Perhaps some may object to this use of the term "psychic" and "spiritual," but I am using them here in their Gnostic meanings.

The term "formless mind" is obscure. It represents the Sanskrit *arā pa*, and I here mean by it the power of mind deduced from its forms.

This mind would spiritually cast no "shadow"; it would give its possessor the capacity of seeing round himself, so to say, observing that which was other than himself, for the fundamental principle of mind is to observe that which is not oneself.

Those among the "dead" who possess it, it is easy to believe, can converse and learn and come back (according to the doctrine of re-incarnation) far wiser than those who spend their time encased in selfishness and unable to respond to "external" contacts, except those that happen exactly to match their own, when of course they can hardly be said to be "external." If they are in unison there is not much to be learned.

We have next an exposition of the K~rmic Powers at work in the world.

First, there is the Unmanifest; then the Manifested or Creative Logos, Zeus, in his mode of self-limitation, that is to say, with his counterpart, spouse, power, or syzygy, Necessity.

The daughter of Zeus and Necessity is Adrasteia, the Inevitable (She-from-whom-none-can-escape, literally), the K~rmic Law.

Servants to her are the three great Powers, Punishment (or Retribution), Justice and Fury (or Vengeance).

Thus there are seven great K~rmic Powers in all. This may be said to be the hierarchy of the justice-side of the Logos; the hierarchy of the mercy-side is another, and yet, perchance, the same.

Punishment has Earth assigned to her as her field of operation; to Justice is assigned the realm of Hades. Mystically this Justice may be well thought of as the pure light of conscience, so beautifully named the Virgin of Light, the Judge, in Magian, Gnostic and Manichæan tradition. The Virgin of Light is, I believe, that pure state which gives birth to really unbiassed understanding. It may be said to be man's higher unbiassed impersonal mind shining into his lower mind. The idea of Justice, Purity and Virginity are here all intimately connected.

Vengeance, the third of Adrasteia's ministers, thrusts the incorrigible down "into a state of which we can neither speak nor think," says our seer's guide; for such speech or thought, presumably, would bring its pictures up before the sight of the "single eye." This is evidently the state which the Greeks called Tartarus (*Tar-Tar*), doubtless a loan-word from some other, and perhaps more ancient, tongue; a "double" possessed of a mystic root-meaning for those skilled in the most primitive of all languages, which the Greeks called *onomatopoi' sis*. It corresponds, though very imperfectly, with the Av§ chi of the Brahmans and Buddhists. The word *a-v§ chi* is said to mean "wave-less." In its extreme sense it is the final state into which the irredeemably evil in spiritual wickedness are thrust, until the end of a world-period. It is called waveless, presumably, because it is a state of complete isolation, and is referred to frequently in the *Pistis Sophia*, a Christian Gnostic document with an Egyptian background.

The torments of this Tartarus are set forth graphically later on in our text. With regard to the corrections in Hades, or the Invisible, I would suggest that the inner side of the matter (whatever the outward appearance may be to the seer) is that we live over again all our evil and good deeds, but now with knowledge and understanding.

Realization makes us understand the justice of punishment and reward. We go through the whole thing ourselves, working it out in immediate experience. The light of our own higher consciousness casts our imperfections into deeper shadow. Our thoughts and emotions become objective to us, and the problems are worked out in very convincing dramatic incidents of a most intimate nature, supplied by the kaleidoscopic memory of the pictures of past deeds.

We are stripped naked to ourselves, and hence, to the world of our consciousness we can no longer deceive. This stripping naked is an indispensable condition of progress, and this is why we must be utterly honest with ourselves. We thus may be said in "trampling on the garment of shame" to lose all shame. "Naked we go to the Naked"--that is, to the Pure. It is next to be remembered that in all folk-conceptions of after-death states, and the relation of the living to the dead, the blood-bond is *the* bond. This is, I think, at the bottom of all ancestor-worship. It is the idea of the group-soul, tribe and family. The root-contract is along the line of blood; that is, the kinship of the animal-human soul. Aridæus thus naturally meets with his "ancestors."

The scheme of the "colours of the souls" most probably pertained to the mystery-doctrine or esoteric teaching which was at that date so widely in the Hellenistic world. Thus, referring to Jacob's dream of the white, and spotted, and ring-straked and speckled kine, Philo of Alexandria tells us that this must be taken as an allegory of souls. The first class of souls, he says, is "white."

"The meaning is that when the soul receives the Divine Seed [of the Logos], the first-born births are spotlessly white, like unto the light of utmost purity, to radiance of the greatest brilliance, as though it were the shadowless ray of the sun's beams from the cloudless sky at noon." (*De Som.*, i. 35.)

I might also suggest an analogy from the markings of bird's eggs; the thought-birds that issue from such soul-eggs being of different classes.

I need hardly add for most of my readers, that the colours of the souls and their meanings given in our text agree very closely with the scheme of colours published in a number of modern theosophical works.

In connection with these colours and the purification of souls, Plutarch gives us an interesting piece of information concerning the philosophy and psychology of the doctrine of metempsychosis as held in his day, when he writes:

"The former souls through weakness of reason, and inertia of the contemplative principle are carried down by the practical element to birth as men; while the latter, lacking an instrument for their unbridled lust, long to unite desires to enjoyment and bring them together by means of any body,--for out of body there is for such souls only an imperfect shadow and dream of pleasure, without fulfilment."

The contemplative and practical elements of the soul may be usefully compared with the qualities or modes (*guna's*) of nature which the Indian philosophers characterize respectively as "pure" (s~ *ttvika*--the symbolical colour of which is "white"), and "passionate" (r~ *jasa*--colour "red")--though indeed it is very difficult to find English equivalents for the root-meanings of these Sanskrit terms.

According to Proclus the contemplative (or theoretic) and the practical are the higher and lower tendencies of the rational principle (*logos*). The term "theoretic" has nothing to do with the modern meaning of the word, but is derived from *theoría,* which signifies direct sight or eye-to-eye knowledge--gnosis.

Macrobius tells us further that the former is "ruled by Saturn" and the latter by "Jupiter." According to the mythology, or rather theology, of the Greeks, Kronos (Saturn) was father of Zeus (Jupiter). Zeus may here be said to be the fabricative power of the Logos.

Porphyry, in his Introduction to the philosophy of Plotinus, tells us that the contemplative or theoretic life has three grades of virtues, the highest of which is the ideal or paradigmatic, pertaining to the spiritual (formless) mind alone. These are the Uranic powers latent in man; Uranus being father of Kronos. They transcend the rest of the soul-powers, just as the type or paradigm transcends the image; for the spiritual mind contacts at once and the same time all the essences which are the types of lower things.

The most intractable class of souls are centred in the animal nature; they are dominated by that mode (*guna*), which the Indian philosophers call "dark" (*t~ masa*--colour "black"), and the description of their most characteristic tendency is corroborated by many seers to-day.

When this mode is in the ascendant, then, and only then, it is said, is retrogression into the "nature of an animal" possible; such a soul allies itself with the irrational. The theory of "re-incarnation into animals" is treated at some length in my volumes on Thrice-greatest Hermes, and it is only necessary here, in order to safeguard the philosophical view of the matter, to quote from Proclus:

"But the true reason asserts that though the human soul may be degraded to brutes, it is only to brutes that possess the life suited to such purpose, while the degraded soul is *as it were* vehicled in this *life* [not body], and *bound to it sympathetically.*"

Our story next introduces us to a change of scene, a vision of the Descent into Genesis, the Vortex that carries the souls down to physical birth.

What the meaning of the Bacchic Caves may be I am not able precisely to say. One commentator tells us that there were in Naxos, and on Parnassus, and elsewhere, caves dedicated to Bacchus, "*i.e.,* to mirth and jollity"; and that "the mouths of these caves were of course decked with all of verdure and bloom that could make them charming and attractive." This may be so; but I am more inclined to think that Plutarch, who was an initiated Dionysian, is comparing the vision with the scenic setting of the mystery-rites.

However this may be, others have described something very similar concerning this mystery and that of the Basin later on, as the following picture of what the writer calls "The Mart of the Souls" (see *Theosoph. Rev.,* Mar., 1905) may testify.

"He looked down, and behold a whirlpool swirled and swept unceasingly before him, the brim of which was stained as though with dyes. Above his head hung a mighty upturned chalice, from whose lip drained a measure as of honey; and it seemed to the man that drop by drop fell into the swirl of the pool, and laid itself along the brim. . . .

"The man saw the thin pale flame-shapes gather round the margin of the pool. Behind them crept strange mists and pallid shadows, shapeless, yet holding potential forms;

forms of ripples, of waves, of the strange clouds that lie about the sky at sunset, of all things unearthly, yet which mimic earth. And the shapeless shadows, too, crept down to the lip of the pool. As they reached the edge where the dyed waters leapt, flame and shadow fused and melted into one, and stood a moment fully formed upon the brink. And the man saw through and through each soul as it stood in its winding sheet of mist. Behind, beyond and through the colours of the vesture, running from the honeyed chalice and the dyed waves, up through the shadows round the separate white flames, the man saw past and future linked in the present; the individual life manifest from that which is called its beginning to that which men call the end. So that to him for the moment, as to each soul, all hearts were opened, and from him no secrets were hid. And he saw this knowledge burning in the flame of each.

"Then the shadow-flames circled round the pool as though in a mystic dance, and the sound of them as they drifted by was as the music of a spell. Deeper hues swept from the brim of the pool to the edges of the shadows, and thicker and ever thicker fell the drops of honey from the chalice over them. The shadows took shape and colour before the man, standing for a moment men like himself, and yet unlike. For they stood as men may stand on Judgment Day, victim and priest, judge and sinner, one and the same, each himself, yet each but part of the rest, judging the earth in himself, and himself in the earth. Then the colours thickened, each hue losing its poignant individuality, merging each in each. And as the colours blurred, so grew the forms more dense. And as the density increased, so did each shadow--erstwhile vast--diminish, drawing to its centre, till it seemed to the man that he looked but on a swarm of bees circling round the rims of one gigantic honey pool. The dyed brim seemed to throw out flowers, great petalled blossoms of amber and orange and scarlet and sapphire, reaching from edge to edge of the whirling water. There was the taste and taint of honey in the air."

But to return to the text of our vision; if this mystery be the "way down," equally is it the "way up." It was "the way by which Dionysus ascended to the Gods." Here again, I think, Plutarch refers to a mystery-myth into which he was initiated. Generally, it may be said to refer to the "greater mysteries"--those of "regeneration," the "way up," while the "lesser mysteries," those of "generation," pertain to the "way down."

The young Bacchus, the Iacchos of the Mysteries, after his own ascent, took up his mother to the Gods--the assumption. Semel‘, in giving birth to Bacchus, the son of Zeus (the creative power of the Logos), is said to have been killed, and subsequently restored by her son to life among the Gods, under a changed name. Mystically, the soul is said to "die" in giving birth to itself on this plane. The "child" thus born may in its turn, in the case of one truly regenerate, become the saviour of its "mother," and raise her from the "dead" to spiritual life among the immortals. In Christian Gnostic tradition this was shown forth at great length in the Sophia-mythus or Wisdom-myth. The Christ rescues and raises the fallen and dead Sophia or soul.

Speaking of this Vortex, which is also called Crat‘r (Mixing-bowl) or Basin, Macrobius writes:

"Plato speaks of this in the *Phædo* and says that the soul is dragged back into body, hurried down by a new intoxication, desiring to taste a fresh draught of the overflow of matter; whereby it is weighed down and brought back to earth. The astral Crater of Dionysus is a symbol of this mystery; and this is what the ancients called the River of Lʻthʻ ."

I have treated of these matters at length in the volumes already referred to. It is necessary, however, to remind ourselves that all these mystery-terms may be taken in a number of senses. I have here attempted to suggest only the meaning which seems most suited to the text. The River of Lʻthʻ , or Place of Oblivion, separates all states and planes from one another. Happy he who can remember and cross it safely whenever and wherever it meets him.

The scene again changes, and the vision is that of the "way up" of the seer, the same mystery as before, but from another point of view. For if there is a Plain of Forgetfulness, there is also a Plain of Truth, of which the scene in our vision is a reflection. For Plutarch elsewhere, speaking of the Great Triangle of the Universe, writes:

"The Area of the Triangle is the Common Hearth of all, and is called the Plain of Truth, in which the *logoi* and ideas and paradigms of all things which have been, and which shall be, lie immutable; and the Æon (or Eternity) being round them, Time flows down upon the world like a stream. And the sight and contemplation of these things are possible for the souls of men only once in 10,000 years, should they have lived a virtuous life."

That is to say, I believe, following the tradition of the Pythagoreans, 10 x 10 x 10 x 10,--the completion or perfection (10) of all the possibilities of the Square (4) of matter, as contrasted with the Triangle (3) of spirit.

Plutarch continues (in this I think speaking of what he knew or had been taught):

"And the highest of our initiations here below is only the dream of that true vision and initiation; and the discourses [*sci.*, delivered in the mysteries] have been carefully devised to awaken the memory of the sublime things above, or else are to no purpose."

But to return to our text and the lunar reflection of this eternal Sun-land; the statement that Orpheus had advanced "as far as this" only, must, I think, be taken as an indication of *jalousie de métier*. Plutarch was high priest of Apollo at Delphi and had doubtless a bone of contention to pick either with his Orphic contemporaries or with the Orphic tradition, which had perhaps belittled the Delphic Oracle.

However this may be, this Crater is declared to be the Oracle of Selʻnʻ, the Moon. That is to say, it pertained to all sublunary dreams and visions--"a mixture of the simple and true with the complex and fallacious."

Beyond this Aridæus could not see, for thereafter began the true Light-world, glimpses of which are so marvellously pourtrayed in Gnostic tradition. Aridæus was still bound to the body, and had not yet been made pure, or freed himself from the "world-illusion," as the Hermes-mystics called it.

The Light of the Spiritual Sun streamed from the Supernal Tripod, or Triangle, of the Plain of Truth, through the Bosom of Themis.

Themis is fabled to have been the daughter of Uranus and Gʻ , of Heaven and Earth, the primæval cosmic pair, or syzygy. Themis is Order, Truth, Equity. The tradition of the Delphians was that their Oracle was first possessed by Gʻ , then by Themis (whom antiquity regarded as a very ancient prophetic divinity), and finally by Apollo. Parnassus was their Holy Mount. The whole symbolism, therefore, agrees with many another mystic tradition, in which the Mount of Contemplation must be ascended before the Sunrise can be seen.

But this was not for Aridæus as yet; he could not see, he could only hear--the voice of the Sibyl. Legend supposed that the so-called face of the moon was that of the Sibyl gazing down upon the earth and singing its fate and that of its dwellers as she circled round.

The "prophecies" we must, I suppose, take as we take those of the Jewish Sibyllines; that is, as after the event. The famous eruption of Vesuvius took place in 79 A.D., and this event is said to have been foretold in the Roman Sibylline Books. Dicæarcheia was one of the towns destroyed, afterwards called Puteoli, the modern Puzzuoli.

As Vespasian died of disease and was not assassinated, as were so many of the Emperors, also in 79 A.D., we may perhaps have here an indication of a date terminus of our story, or of the writing of the treatise of Plutarch, if that is of any importance.

The scene next changes to a gruesome vision of the inferno, where it is to be noted that his terror deprived the seer of the presence of his "gentle and familiar guide," and immersed him in all the horrors of the infernal living picture-gallery.

The idea of being turned "inside-out" in the after-state is graphically compared with the sea-polyps or scolopendra, a fish that was supposed by the ancients to have the power occasionally of throwing out its intestines. When caught by a hook it was fabled to eject its entrails, remove the hook and then take them in again--an excellent "Philologic" romance, that does not, however, seem to have come down to the mediæval Bestiaries.

When used of the soul it suggests that the "inner" became as the "outer," and the "outer" as the "inner." That is to say, in earth-life the modes of passion are ever changing, while the external form remains the same; whereas in this state of soul-life, the ruling modes of passion are more constant and the external forms are ever changing. In other words, the passions may be said to objectivize themselves, in that they immediately work out or clothe themselves in appropriate forms.

We next come to the "lakes" of the inferno, there being three of them, the root-number of the tradition in which our vision has its setting. The "lakes" and the alchemical processes suggest that the background of the whole picture had its original in Egypt.

The scene appears to depict symbolically the preparation of degenerate souls prior to their being vehicled in the "life of an animal." From the standpoint of mystic psychology this concerns the "configuration" of the passional nature, or that nature which man shares with the animal, and may be said to be connected with types of mind that may be classified by parallels drawn from the types of animals, the lords of which are the "sacred animals."

The allusion to Nero is, of course, topical and again affords an indication of date.

What "Pindar's viper," or a "Pindaric viper" may mean is hard to say. It is most natural to suppose that we have here reference to some famous comparison of the great poet's, and that the ode which contained it is now lost.

It refers, of course, to Nero's guilt of matricide; while the "creature that croaks" is a humorous allusion to the Emperor's vanity and his appearing in the theatre as a singer. It is, however, not true that Nero freed Greece; he freed the province of Achæia only from taxes.

Who the "woman of amazing form and size" may be, I cannot divine, unless she be Memory, the counterpart of the Scribe of the Gods. Encaustic painters, as they were called, burnt in the colours with a heated rod or stylus.

Aridæus returned to his body by way of a "vortex," even as he went forth in the manner of a "bubble."

In conclusion I would suggest that the story of the experiences of Aridæus is either a literary subterfuge for describing part of the instruction in certain mysteries, or the vision, in popular story-form, was considered so true a description of what was thought to be the nature of the invisible world and the after-death conditions of the soul, that it required little alteration to make it useful for that purpose.

It is further interesting to notice that one of the characters in Plato's Vision of Er is called Ardiæus, while in Plutarch the main personage is called Aridæus. The transposition of a single letter is so slight as to make the names practically identical, and the subject matter is so similar that one is inclined to think there must be some connection between these two famous visions. Moreover Aridæus is said to have been a native of Soli in Cilicia, just as Er is said to have been a Pamphylian; the tradition of both stories would then seem to have been derived from Asia Minor, and the origin of them may be hidden in the syncretism of that land--where West and East were for ever meeting. Our story would thus seem to be intended to give the reader an idea of the impression made on the mind of one whom Plutarch would have us consider one of the uninitiated, by the Vision of Hades, or of the Invisible World, "as far as the moon." Sopat' r of Apamea also tells us the story of a young man who had seen the mysteries in a dream and had to be initiated afterwards.

We are told that Aridæus returned to his body before undergoing some process whereby he might "the better remember the details." What he remembered, therefore, is confused, clothed in the language and symbols of the mythologic recitals with which he was acquainted. Had Aridæus been really initiated, he would probably not have been represented as requiring a guide, and would have remembered everything clearly without the cloaking of images reflected from physical forms, and of scenery created by the recitals of popular religion, or the dramatic setting of formal mystery-rites.

Printed in Great Britain
by Amazon